# Awesome Animal Adventures

Pauline Cartwright

## Contents

# Awesome Animal Adventure

Hi there! My name is Dr. Dig and I think animals are **awesome**.

I'm going to take you on an adventure through time. We're going to learn about some of the biggest animals that ever lived. We're even going to see the **biggest** animal of all time! Can you guess what it is?

*Tyrannosaurus rex*

*Giant Sloth*

*African Elephant*

# Giants of the Past

If we really want to find out about giant animals, we have to go way, way back – to the time of the dinosaurs. Dinosaurs lived between 65 and 230 million years ago. Some dinosaurs were small, but many **species** of dinosaur were among the largest animals that ever lived.

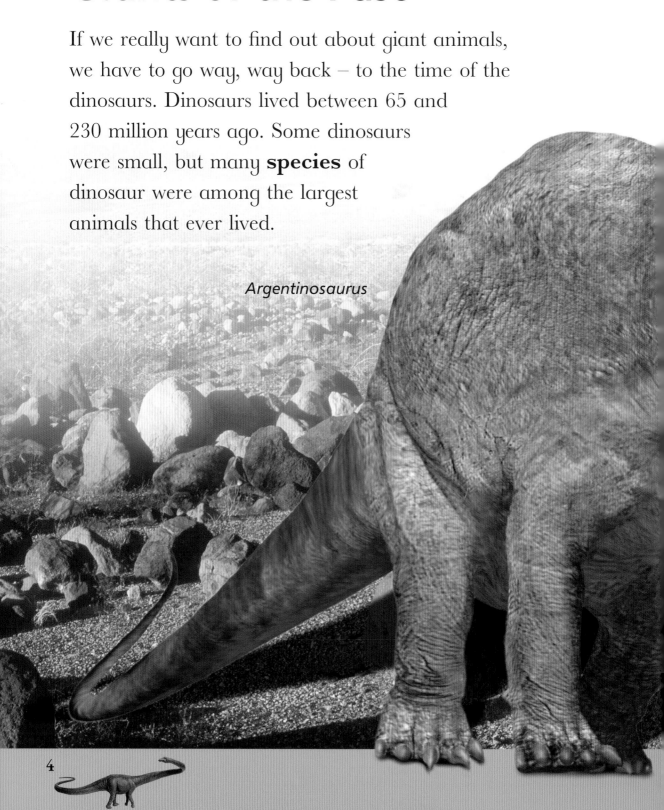

*Argentinosaurus*

## Argentinosaurus

The biggest dinosaur we know of was the Argentinosaurus. Argentinosaurus lived about 95 million years ago. It was a long dinosaur – even longer than four buses parked end-to-end. Argentinosaurus' bones were found in Argentina, in South America.

**EXTINCT**

**Argentinosaurus**

| | |
|---|---|
| Size: | 35 m long |
| Weight: | 90 tonnes |
| Food: | plants |
| Lifespan: | may have been 50 – 100 years |

*This dinosaur is BIG!*

## Sauropods

Argentinosaurus was a sauropod.
All sauropods ate plants. They
had very long necks and long tails.
Sauropods were the largest animals
ever to live on land.

*Barosaurus was
also a sauropod.*

Argentinosaurus was the biggest animal ever to walk on Earth! But it's not the biggest animal of all time. Keep reading …

60 cm

0 cm

> ### Crack the Whip!
> Some sauropods may have cracked their long tails like whips. This would have made a sound like thunder! This would scare away any likely **predators**.

This is just one part of an Argentinosaurus's backbone!

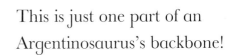

# Spinosaurus

The largest meat-eating dinosaur we know of was Spinosaurus. Spinosaurus lived between 93.5 – 119 million years ago. Its back spines were the size of a tall man! These spines may have been covered with skin – just like a sail on a boat.

**EXTINCT**

## Spinosaurus

Size: 18 m long

Weight: 9 tonnes

Food: meat

Lifespan: about 40 years

### Scary!

The spiny "sail" on Spinosaurus might have scared away attackers. It made Spinosaurus look even bigger than it already was!

# Tyrannosaurus rex

Tyrannosaurus rex is one of the most famous dinosaurs. It may not have been the biggest, but it was still a giant.

Tyrannosaurus rex lived between 65 and 68 million years ago. T. rex looked fierce, but it may not have been a great hunter. Some scientists believe that it may have been a **scavenger**, eating animals that were already dead. It's impossible to know for sure!

*Wow!*

## What's in a Name?

Tyrannosaurus rex's name means, "tyrant lizard king".

EXTINCT

**Tyrannosaurus rex**

Size:        13 m long

Weight:    7 tonnes

Food:       meat

Lifespan: about 30 years

# The End of the Dinosaurs

The last of the dinosaurs died about 65 million years ago. Scientists believe that an **asteroid** may have crashed into Earth. This would have caused lots of dust and clouds to block out the sun for many years. Without warmth and light, the dinosaurs couldn't survive.

But that didn't mean the end of giant animals.

*Next stop on the tour ... mammals!*

# Mammoth Mammals!

After the dinosaurs died, more and more species of mammals **evolved**. Most of these mammals were small, but many were enormous.

The woolly rhinoceros could grow up to 2 m tall with a 1 m long front horn.

## Giant Rhinoceros

You've probably seen pictures of a rhinoceros. They're pretty big, aren't they? But scientists have found a **fossil** of an enormous rhinoceros that lived 25 million years ago.

The early rhinoceros doesn't look much like the rhino we know today. For a start, it doesn't have any horns on its nose. And that long neck looks like it belongs on a giraffe.

*Modern-day rhinoceros*

*Say hello to your cousin!*

## Early Rhinoceros

| | |
|---|---|
| Size: | 5.5 m tall at shoulder |
| Weight: | 10 – 20 tonnes |
| Food: | plants |
| Lifespan: | unknown |

# Woolly Mammoth

The woolly mammoth is a cousin of the elephant. It lived during the **Ice Age**, when it was very cold. It had a thick coat of fur, which would have come in handy.

Woolly mammoths' tusks were longer and more curved than those of the elephant. Mammoths may have used their tusks to push ice and snow out of their way.

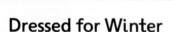

### Dressed for Winter

The mammoth's thick fur coat was made up of two layers of hair. Below that was a thick layer of fat.

## Woolly Mammoth

| | |
|---|---|
| Size: | 4 – 5m tall at shoulder |
| Weight: | 8 tonnes |
| Food: | plants |
| Lifespan: | about 60 – 80 years |

It's freezing! May I borrow your coat?

Mammoths became **extinct** 9000 years ago. So how do we know about them? Scientists have found whole mammoths frozen in ice. The ice **preserves** the body. Some mammoth bodies have been so well preserved that we can still see their fur and eyelashes.

*This is Dima, a baby woolly mammoth.*
*It was frozen in ice for 40 000 years!*

## In Search of Food

Like elephants today, woolly mammoths travelled in herds.
They roamed the land eating grasses, flowers and leaves.

# Giant Ground Sloth

The word "sloth" means slow, or lazy. Sloths today spend most of their time hanging from trees, and only move when they have to.

But during the Ice Age, sloths were very different. These animals were huge – even bigger than an elephant. In fact, they were the biggest mammals ever to live on land.

## Walking Tall

The Giant ground sloth spent a lot of time walking on two feet, a bit like a bear. Just imagine – an animal bigger than an elephant walking on two legs!

EXTINCT

Giant Sloth

Size: 6 m long

Weight: 3.8 tonnes

Food: plants

Lifespan: unknown

Next stop the present day!

# Giants Among Us

Here we are, back in the present day. There are plenty of giants left for us to see – including the biggest animal of all time! But let's take a look at these other giants first.

## The African Elephant

There are two types of elephant, African and Asian. The African elephant is the larger of the two. It is the biggest land animal today.

**ALIVE**

African Elephant

Size:     3 – 4 m tall at shoulder

Weight:   3 – 6 tonnes

Food:     plants

Lifespan: about 70 years

**What's the Difference?**
African elephants have much bigger ears than Asian elephants. They have a dip in their back, and their tusks are usually larger than those of Asian elephants.

*I have met your cousin!*

# Colossal Squid

The colossal squid is one of the largest animals in the ocean. It has a large reddish-pink body, with arms and **tentacles** about 2 metres long.

The colossal squid has sharp hooks at the ends of its arms and tentacles. These hooks can cause serious injuries to the whales that like to eat squid!

## All the Better to See You With!

The colossal squid has eyes that are as big as footballs.

Gulp!

### Colossal Squid

Size: 12 – 14 m

Weight: around 450 kg

Food: large fish and other squid

Lifespan: unknown

ALIVE

# The Biggest Ever!

Here we are, at the end of our tour. And we've kept the biggest until last. The biggest animal on Earth lives in the ocean. It's the blue whale.

## The Blue Whale

The blue whale is not just the biggest animal alive today – it's the biggest animal that has ever lived!

It's even bigger than Argentinosaurus. The blue whale's tongue alone weighs as much as an elephant!

A newborn whale is
8 metres long.

**Blue Whale**

Size:        33 m long

Weight:   up to 180 tonnes

Food:       krill and other small
                 marine animals

Lifespan: 85 years

# Big Appetite, Tiny Food!

The blue whale may be the biggest animal, but its favourite food is one of the smallest. Krill are very tiny shrimps about the size of a jellybean! A hungry blue whale can eat 3 tonnes of krill a day which is about the same weight as six cows.

krill

## Coming up for Air

Whales are mammals, not fish. They can dive 500 metres, but must come up to the surface to breathe. The blue whale can stay under water for about 30 minutes.

Blue whales have **baleen plates** – a kind of **filter** made of the same stuff as your fingernails. The whale gulps a mouthful of seawater then pushes it back out through the baleen. All the krill and other small creatures get left behind for the whale to swallow.

baleen plates

# Just Imagine ...

Many of the animals we've seen today are extinct. But imagine sharing our streets with a woolly mammoth, or a Giant sloth! It's probably just as well we're never likely to meet Spinosaurus or Tyrannosaurus rex ... but it's still fun to imagine a world in which they're still alive!

Well, that's it – the end of our tour! I hope you've enjoyed it as much as I have.

# Glossary

**awesome**
amazing, wonderful

**asteroid**
piece of rock or metal, in space, that moves around the Sun

**baleen plates**
bony but springy plates that hang from a whale's jaw

**evolved**
changed slowly over time

**extinct**
when a species of animal or plant dies out

**filter**
something used to stop small particles mixing with air or water

**fossil**
remains of plants and animals that lived a long time ago

**Ice Age**
time in the past when much of Earth was covered in ice and snow

**mammals**
warm-blooded animals that produce milk for their young

**predators**
animals that hunt and eat other animals

**preserves**
keeps in good condition

**scavenger**
an animal that feeds on dead animals

**species**
group of animals that are alike

**tentacles**
long, flexible body parts used for gripping